DISABILITIES CAN'T STOP US!

HELEN KELLER

An Impulse to Soar

Caitie McAneney

PowerKiDS press

New York

Published in 2021 by The Rosen Publishing Group, Inc.
29 East 21st Street, New York, NY 10010

First Edition

Editor: Elizabeth Krajnik
Book Design: Reann Nye

Photo Credits: Cover Hulton Archive/Archive Photos/Getty Images; series art (background) Ratana21/Shutterstock.com; p. 5 https://commons.wikimedia.org/wiki/File:Helen_Keller_circa_1920_-_restored.jpg; pp. 7, 9, 13, 25, 27 Bettmann/Getty Images;
p. 11 Historical/Corbis Historical/Getty Images; p. 15 Topical Press Agency/Hulton Archive/Getty Images; pp. 17, 19 Courtesy of the Library of Congress; p. 21 Buyenlarge/Archive Photos/Getty Images; p. 23 PA Images/Getty Images; p. 29 Time Life Pictures/The LIFE Picture Collection/Getty Images.

Cataloging-in-Publication Data

Names: McAneney, Caitie.
Title: Helen Keller: an impulse to soar / Caitie McAneney.
Description: New York : PowerKids Press, 2021. | Series: Disabilities can't stop us! | Includes glossary and index.
Identifiers: ISBN 9781725311145 (pbk.) | ISBN 9781725311169 (library bound) | ISBN 9781725311152 (6 pack)
Subjects: LCSH: Keller, Helen, 1880-1968–Juvenile literature. | Sullivan, Annie, 1866-1936–Juvenile literature. | Deafblind women–United States–Biography–Juvenile literature. | Deafblind people–United States–Biography–Juvenile literature.
Classification: LCC HV1624.K4 M39 2020 | DDC 362.4'1092 B–dc23

Manufactured in the United States of America

CPSIA Compliance Information: Batch #CSPK20. For Further Information contact Rosen Publishing, New York, New York at 1-800-237-9932.

CONTENTS

Against All Odds 4
A Life-Changing Illness.................. 6
Out of Options.............................. 8
A Tremendous Teacher..................10
A Hunger for Education.................12
College Bound!.............................14
Telling Her Story 16
An Amazing Advocate 18
Helen in the Spotlight...................20
Around the World 22
A Special Spokesperson................24
The Highest Honors..................... 26
The Greatest Woman of Our Age 28
Timeline.......................................30
Glossary......................................31
Index...32
Websites 32

Against All Odds

Helen Keller lived an amazing life as a writer, public speaker, and **advocate** for people with disabilities. By any standards, she was extraordinary in her works. However, what makes her a hero to many, as well as a symbol of **resilience**, is the fact that she was both deaf and blind.

Even though she died more than 50 years ago, Keller is still well known. This is because she overcame very steep odds to achieve her dreams. Even though she couldn't hear people speak or see words on paper, she learned to communicate in a way that allowed the whole world to hear her story. With a strong will, she unlocked her voice and showed the world her intelligence and ability.

One of Helen Keller's most famous quotes is, "One cannot consent to creep when one feels an impulse to soar."

Blindness in History

For much of history, blind people couldn't go to school. In 1784, Valentin Haüy established the first school for the blind in Paris, France. He also developed a raised alphabet system so people with blindness could read. In 1831, the Perkins School for the Blind opened in Boston, Massachusetts. It wasn't until 1975 that education for the blind became a right. Today, many blind people attend **integrated** schools.

A Life-Changing Illness

Helen Keller was born on June 27, 1880, in Tuscumbia, Alabama. She was an extremely intelligent baby, and her parents said she was already trying to speak before she was one year old. However, when she was around 19 months old, Keller's life took a turn.

Keller became very sick with a fever, and it looked like she might die. Today, people think it may have been meningitis or scarlet fever—both life-threatening diseases. While Keller did survive, she lost her ability to see and hear. Dark, silent years followed for Keller. Her parents didn't know what to do for her. She tried communicating with basic hand motions and touching people's lips. However, this often led to **frustration** for Keller.

Keller's disabilities often made it hard for her to communicate with others. However, she said she had two great friends in her childhood—her dog Belle and a cook's daughter named Martha Washington.

Out of Options

Keller's frustrations often led to outbursts of anger. In her **autobiography**, *The Story of My Life*, Keller wrote, "I do not remember when I first realized that I was different from other people, but I knew it before my teacher came to me."

She remembered knowing other people moved their lips to communicate and feeling "vexed," or troubled, by it. That led to kicking and screaming on her part.

Keller's parents wanted to find her the best opportunities possible, but there were few choices. There were schools for children with sight and hearing loss, but they were far away. At that time, it was also uncertain whether someone deaf and blind could be taught. A special doctor in Baltimore, Maryland, couldn't help her eyesight. It seemed they were out of options.

Laura Bridgman was proof that people who were both deaf and blind could learn to communicate.

A School for the Blind

In the 1800s, few schools were suited to teach people who were blind and deaf. After their trip to Baltimore, Keller's parents wrote to the Perkins School for the Blind to find a teacher for Helen. The Perkins School for the Blind, originally called the New England Asylum for the Blind, was the first of its kind. It took on its first deaf and blind student—a girl named Laura Bridgman—in 1837. Bridgman's success at Perkins was a source of hope for Keller's parents.

A Tremendous Teacher

In the end, the Kellers' trip to Baltimore was a success after all. The Perkins School was able to find her a teacher—Anne Sullivan. Keller said the day Sullivan arrived to teach her was the most important day of her life. To this day, Sullivan is regarded as one of the most inspirational teachers to ever live.

Sullivan had her work cut out for her. Because Helen lost her sight and hearing at such a young age, she had no vocabulary, or words. Sullivan tried to teach Keller words through a **manual alphabet**, but Keller couldn't connect them with actual objects. Then, one day, Sullivan led Keller out to a water pump, and signed the word "water" into Keller's hand while pumping the water. Suddenly, Keller understood—the sign meant water. This breakthrough paved the way for the rest of Keller's education.

UNSTOPPABLE!

Due to a childhood illness, Anne Sullivan also had vision loss, and she couldn't read or write until the age of 14 when she entered the Perkins School.

At the Perkins School, Sullivan became friends with Bridgman. From Bridgman, she learned skills that would help her teach Keller later on.

Alexander Graham Bell

Alexander Graham Bell is best known for his most famous invention, the telephone. However, he also worked to help those with hearing loss. In fact, Keller's parents sought help from Bell on their trip to Baltimore, and he connected them to the Perkins School, which connected them to Anne Sullivan. Keller and Bell were friends for many years, and she even attended the World's Fair with him in 1893. There, he taught Keller about how telephones, phonographs, and autophones worked.

A Hunger for Education

Once Keller understood how words and objects were connected, the world opened up to her. After much time and practice, she was able to communicate.

In her autobiography, Keller recounted the day she realized her first **abstract** thought. It was hard for her to make sense of things she couldn't touch. Later, when Keller was struggling with a lesson, Sullivan spelled "think" against her forehead. Keller understood that this was the word for what she was doing—thinking about the problem. Then, she thought about "love" in the same way and began to understand.

Keller then learned how to read, feeling for raised letters with her fingers. Books for the blind are usually written in **Braille**. Reading opened Keller up to new ways of learning.

Keller learned to "lip-read" with her fingers. She would place her thumb on the speaker's throat, index finger on their upper lip, and middle finger on their nose to feel vibrations and learn words.

Learning to Speak

Learning to speak was a new challenge for Keller. When she was around 10, she started studying with a teacher named Sarah Fuller. Fuller would let Keller put her hands on her face as she spoke different sounds. Keller learned by the vibration of her throat, expression of her face, and movements of her mouth. Sullivan practiced speech with Keller tirelessly, even as Keller's words were far from perfect. Keller recalled repeating, "I am not [silent] now!" excitedly out loud.

College Bound!

Keller had a dream—to go to college. She first had to study very hard and with more challenges than any of her classmates. In 1888, she started classes at the Perkins School for the Blind in Boston, Massachusetts. In 1894, she moved to New York City to attend the Wright-Humason School for the Deaf. There she studied math, geography, French, and German.

Keller wanted to go to Radcliffe College, but first she had to prepare at Cambridge School for Young Ladies. These classes weren't taught for students with hearing or vision loss, so Keller had to work extra hard to understand lectures, assignments, and exams. Her teachers worried she would push herself to a breaking point, but she wouldn't give up. Her hard work paid off, and she got into Radcliffe College.

UNSTOPPABLE!

Keller's toughest subject was math. She often didn't have the resources to learn it properly. For example, she couldn't see how different parts of shapes related to one another.

To take an exam at Cambridge, Keller would type her answers on a typewriter. Then, she'd have someone read it back to her using a manual alphabet so she could check for errors. At Radcliffe, she wouldn't be able to have someone read papers back to her, and she could only make changes to errors if there was time to spare during the examination period.

Telling Her Story

It was clear that Keller had an amazing life that could be inspiring to others—she'd grown from a child that people thought couldn't be taught to a young woman with a college education.

Keller was hesitant to tell her story to the world. However, in time, she chose to tell her story anyway. In 1903, during her years at Radcliffe, she published her most famous work—*The Story of My Life*.

This autobiography covered her life from her childhood until the time she started college at Radcliffe. She wrote about her struggles before she learned how to communicate, her challenges and joys learning about the world, and her relationship with Anne Sullivan.

UNSTOPPABLE!

Keller published many books, including *The World I Live In*, *Out of the Dark*, *My Religion*, *Helen Keller's Journal*, and *Teacher.*

Keller's autobiography was first published as a series of stories in *Ladies' Home Journal*. It was made into a book, translated into many languages, and sold worldwide.

An Accusation of Plagiarism

Keller was nervous to tell her story because of an experience with **plagiarism**. When Keller was at Perkins School for the Blind, she wrote a story called "The Frost King." It was published in a magazine, but the director of the school found out that it had been plagiarized. Keller never meant to plagiarize—she'd just forgotten that she'd heard the story before. She was deeply scarred from the experience, and she was afraid to ever write again.

An Amazing Advocate

In 1904, Keller graduated from Radcliffe College with honors. She was the first deaf and blind person to finish college, and she wanted to advocate for others. She talked about her disability and spoke out on behalf of other people. Subjects important to her included women's right to vote, worker's rights, and **socialism**.

Keller advocated for easier reading materials for people with vision loss. When Keller was learning to read and write, there were many different systems of raised-letter writing. A person would have to learn different systems to read different books. Keller wanted Braille to be more widely used and accessible for people with vision loss. Because of Keller's work, Braille became the single writing system for people with vision loss in the United States in 1918.

UNSTOPPABLE!

Keller spoke in front of the U.S. Congress to advocate for people with vision loss. She said blind people deserved a better quality of life.

Graduating from Radcliffe College was a major achievement for Keller. It meant she could soar just as high as other people.

Helen in the Spotlight

Keller quickly became a celebrity as she spoke to larger audiences. Even though she was very self-conscious about her speaking voice, she still put herself on view to show the world that people with disabilities could do anything they put their mind to.

In 1919, the silent film *Deliverance* told Keller's story. Keller and Sullivan acted as themselves in the movie. The same year, Keller also started her career in vaudeville.

Vaudeville is a kind of stage entertainment that was made up of a bunch of short, usually funny, acts. It was popular between the 1890s and 1930s in the United States. Keller would answer questions from the audience about her life and politics in a funny way.

UNSTOPPABLE!

Keller's political views were also in the spotlight. The Federal Bureau of Investigation (FBI) watched her for her support of socialist leaders.

Keller and Sullivan went on lecture tours around the United States. Sullivan interpreted Keller's speech for the audience, and both women would answer the audience's questions. However, these tours were exhausting for Sullivan.

Around the World

Keller became a well-known speaker, giving lectures at medical schools, colleges, and organizations for the blind. Between 1919 and 1924, she traveled around the United States, spreading her story and advocating for the education of people with disabilities. She was living proof that people could be educated even if they were deaf, blind, or both.

Keller's fame also took her around the world, from Europe to the Middle East to Asia. In 1946, she started touring the world for 11 years, a time in which she traveled to 35 countries. While there, she spoke with the most important political leaders in the world—including prime ministers and presidents. This inspired many leaders to establish or deepen their educational opportunities for people with disabilities.

UNSTOPPABLE!

Anne Sullivan died in 1936. Keller no longer had her teacher by her side, but she continued to make appearances and travel.

Helen Keller

Polly Thomson

Keller's travel companion on her world tours was her close friend and secretary, Polly Thomson.

A Special Spokesperson

Keller worked with and for many foundations and organizations that worked to improve the lives of people with disabilities. She was one of the founding members of the Massachusetts Commission for the Blind, established in 1906. The commission worked to provide services for blind people.

In 1924, she became a spokesperson, or speaker, for the American Foundation for the Blind (AFB). The AFB was founded to make sure people with vision loss get the services and education they need to live productive lives. Keller worked with the AFB for more than 40 years. She was their counselor on national and international relations, which meant she traveled the world on behalf of the organization. When Keller died, she left her papers, letters, and photographs to the AFB.

UNSTOPPABLE!

Helen Keller International is an organization inspired by Keller's work with soldiers blinded in World War I. Today, the organization works to prevent blindness and help people with vision loss.

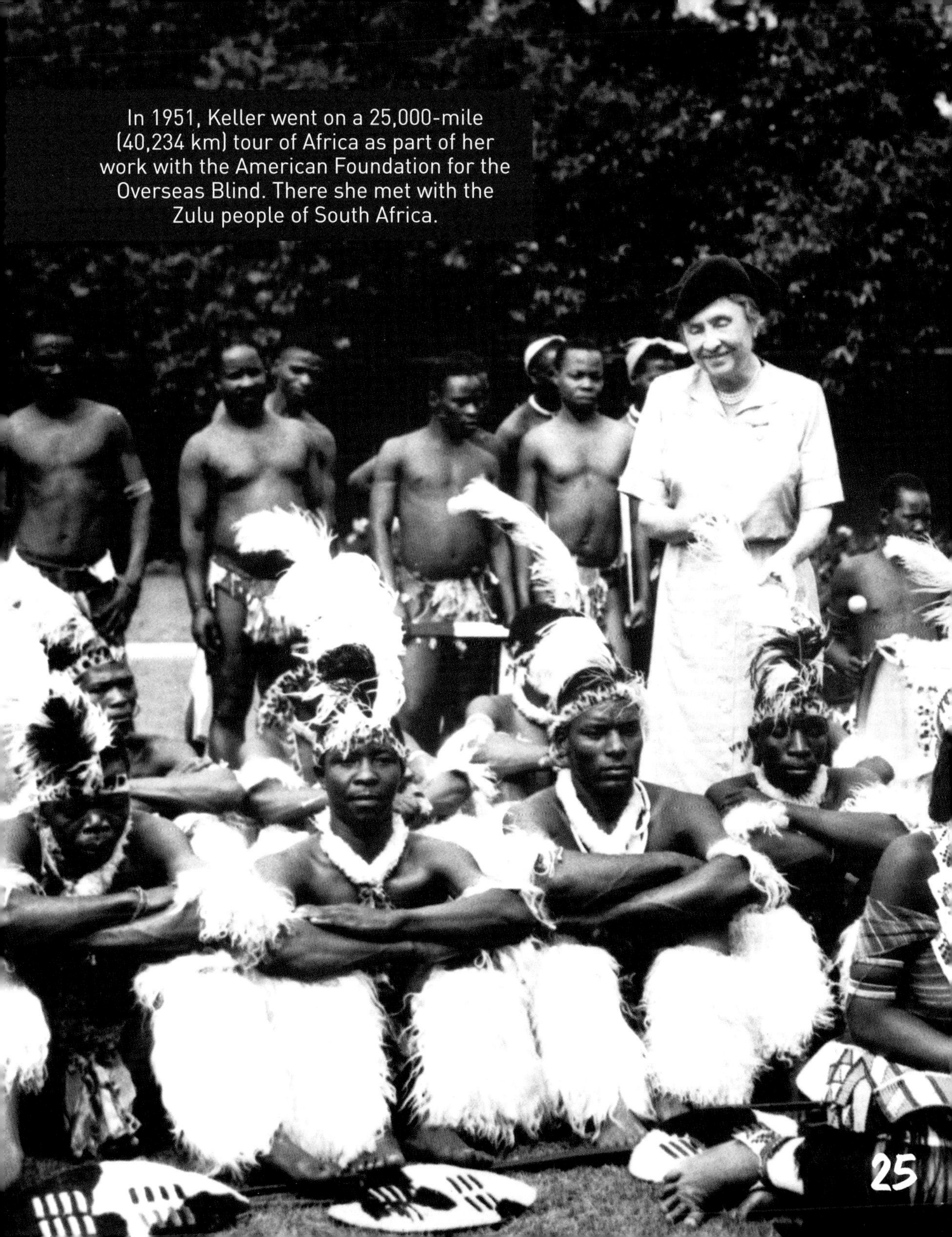
In 1951, Keller went on a 25,000-mile (40,234 km) tour of Africa as part of her work with the American Foundation for the Overseas Blind. There she met with the Zulu people of South Africa.

The Highest Honors

Helen Keller's work for people with vision and hearing loss was **unprecedented**. She was a household name, famous around the world for her amazing story and her work as an advocate for people with disabilities.

She was inducted, or added, to the Women's Hall of Fame in 1973, a few years after her death. She was also awarded the Lions Humanitarian Award from Lions Club International, an organization that helps people with vision loss. She met 12 presidents in her lifetime, from Grover Cleveland to John F. Kennedy. In 1964, President Lyndon B. Johnson awarded her the Presidential Medal of Freedom, which is one of the highest civilian awards in the United States, for her great work and impact on the nation.

Keller met and became friends with some of the most **influential** people in America, including Alexander Graham Bell, Mark Twain, and Eleanor Roosevelt.

Eleanor Roosevelt

Helen Keller

The Greatest Woman of Our Age

Helen Keller died on June 1, 1968. In her 87 years, she changed the world's view of people with disabilities and worked to provide services, respect, and education to these people. Her childhood illness and disability could have held her back from living a full life, but Helen had an impulse to soar—and soar she did.

British Prime Minister Winston Churchill once called Keller, "The greatest woman of our age." As a supporter of worker's rights, disability rights, civil rights, and women's voting rights, among other causes, Keller's impact on the world is unlike any other. She is quoted as saying, "The only thing worse than being blind is having sight but no vision." Without a doubt, it was Keller's vision that truly changed the world.

Helen Keller is often quoted as saying, "The best and most beautiful things in the world cannot be seen or even touched—they must be felt with the heart."

TIMELINE

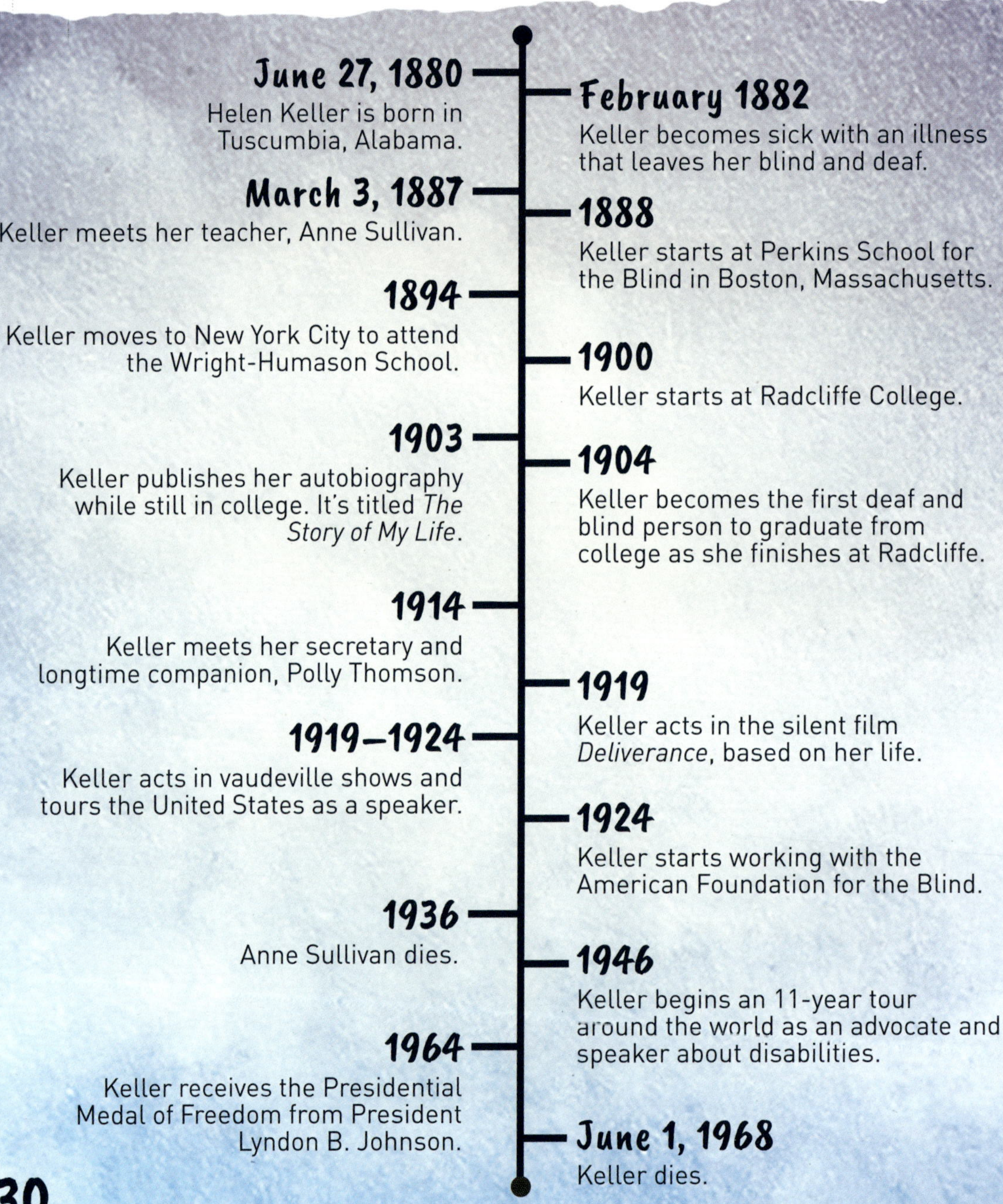

June 27, 1880
Helen Keller is born in Tuscumbia, Alabama.

February 1882
Keller becomes sick with an illness that leaves her blind and deaf.

March 3, 1887
Keller meets her teacher, Anne Sullivan.

1888
Keller starts at Perkins School for the Blind in Boston, Massachusetts.

1894
Keller moves to New York City to attend the Wright-Humason School.

1900
Keller starts at Radcliffe College.

1903
Keller publishes her autobiography while still in college. It's titled *The Story of My Life*.

1904
Keller becomes the first deaf and blind person to graduate from college as she finishes at Radcliffe.

1914
Keller meets her secretary and longtime companion, Polly Thomson.

1919
Keller acts in the silent film *Deliverance*, based on her life.

1919–1924
Keller acts in vaudeville shows and tours the United States as a speaker.

1924
Keller starts working with the American Foundation for the Blind.

1936
Anne Sullivan dies.

1946
Keller begins an 11-year tour around the world as an advocate and speaker about disabilities.

1964
Keller receives the Presidential Medal of Freedom from President Lyndon B. Johnson.

June 1, 1968
Keller dies.

GLOSSARY

abstract: Expressing a quality apart from an object.

advocate: A person who argues for or supports a cause or policy. Also, to support or argue for a cause or policy.

autobiography: A book that tells the story of a person's life that is written by the person it is about.

Braille: A system of writing for the blind that uses characters made up of raised dots.

frustration: A feeling of anger or annoyance caused by being unable to do something.

influential: Having a great influence, or effect, on something or someone.

integrated: Part of a larger group.

manual alphabet: An alphabet especially for the deaf in which the letters are represented by finger positions.

plagiarism: The act of copying the ideas or words of another person without giving credit to that person.

resilience: The ability to recover from or overcome great misfortune or change.

socialism: A social system or theory in which the government owns and controls the means of production and distribution of goods.

unprecedented: Not done or experienced before.

INDEX

A
American Foundation for the Blind (AFB), 24, 30

B
Bell, Alexander Graham, 11, 26
Boston, 5, 14, 30
Braille, 12, 18
Bridgman, Laura, 8, 9, 11

C
Cambridge School for Young Ladies, 14, 15
Churchill, Winston, 28
Cleveland, Grover, 26
Congress, U.S., 18

D
Deliverance, 20, 30

F
Fuller, Sarah, 13

H
Haüy, Valentin, 5
Helen Keller International, 24
Helen Keller's Journal, 16

J
Johnson, Lyndon B., 26, 30

K
Kennedy, John F., 26

M
My Religion, 16

O
Out of the Dark, 16

P
Perkins School for the Blind, 5, 9, 10, 11, 14, 17, 30
Presidential Medal of Freedom, 26, 30

R
Radcliffe College, 14, 15, 16, 18, 19, 30
Roosevelt, Eleanor, 26, 27

S
Story of My Life, The, 8, 16, 30
Sullivan, Anne, 10, 11, 12, 13, 16, 20, 21, 22, 30

T
Teacher, 16
Thomson, Polly, 23, 30
Twain, Mark, 26

W
Women's Hall of Fame, 26
World I Live In, The, 16
Wright-Humason School for the Deaf, 14, 30

WEBSITES

Due to the changing nature of Internet links, PowerKids Press has developed an online list of websites related to the subject of this book. This site is updated regularly. Please use this link to access the list: www.powerkidslinks.com/dcsu/keller